WHAT IS MY

KITCHEN

MADE OF?

Written by
ALEX HALL

MATERIALS AT HOME

Library of Congress Control Number:
The Library of Congress Control Number is available on the Library of Congress website.

ISBN
979-8-89359-430-0 (library bound)
979-8-89359-450-8 (paperback)
979-8-89359-488-1 (epub)
979-8-89359-470-6 (hosted ebook)

Printed in the United States of America
Mankato, MN
012026

sales@northstareditions.com
888-417-0195

Written by:
Alex Hall

Edited by:
Noah Leatherland

Designed by:
Amy Li

All facts, statistics, web addresses, and URLs in this book were verified as valid and accurate at time of writing. No responsibility for any changes to external websites or references can be accepted by either the author or publisher.

PHOTO CREDITS

ALL IMAGES ARE COURTESY OF SHUTTERSTOCK.COM, UNLESS OTHERWISE STATED.
Recurring – fire_fly. xnova. Cover – Kitchen_Boycutout. MC_Noppadol. mStudioVector. New Africa. Queenmoonlite Studio. 4–5 – Phawat. Yuganov Konstantin. 6–7 – Pixel-Shot. Robert Golebiewski. HenadziPechan. Aleksei Golovanov. 8–9 – Pixel-Shot. noprati somchit. HTeam. 10–11 – Michael C. Gray. RHJPhtotos. JasminkaM. 12–13 – New Africa. valzan. JLco Julia Amaral. 14–15 – cherezoff. Vitaly Korovin. New Africa. 16–17 – Louella938. Oleg Opryshko. Elizabeth A. Cummings. 18–19 – HAKINMHAN. Regreto. JeannieR. 20–21 – Niik Leuangboriboon. Fotofermer. Spalnic. Taras Kvakush. FabrikaSimf. photo_journey. 22–23 – BM_27. Q88.

CONTENTS

Words that look like **this** can be found in the glossary on page 24.

WHAT ARE MATERIALS?

There are many things that you can see and touch in your kitchen. These things are known as objects. Objects are made of materials. Some materials are made by humans. Others are natural.

Metals are found in the ground.

Every material has properties. Properties are ways of describing what something is like. Some materials are rough and hard. Others are smooth and soft. Different properties make materials good at different jobs.

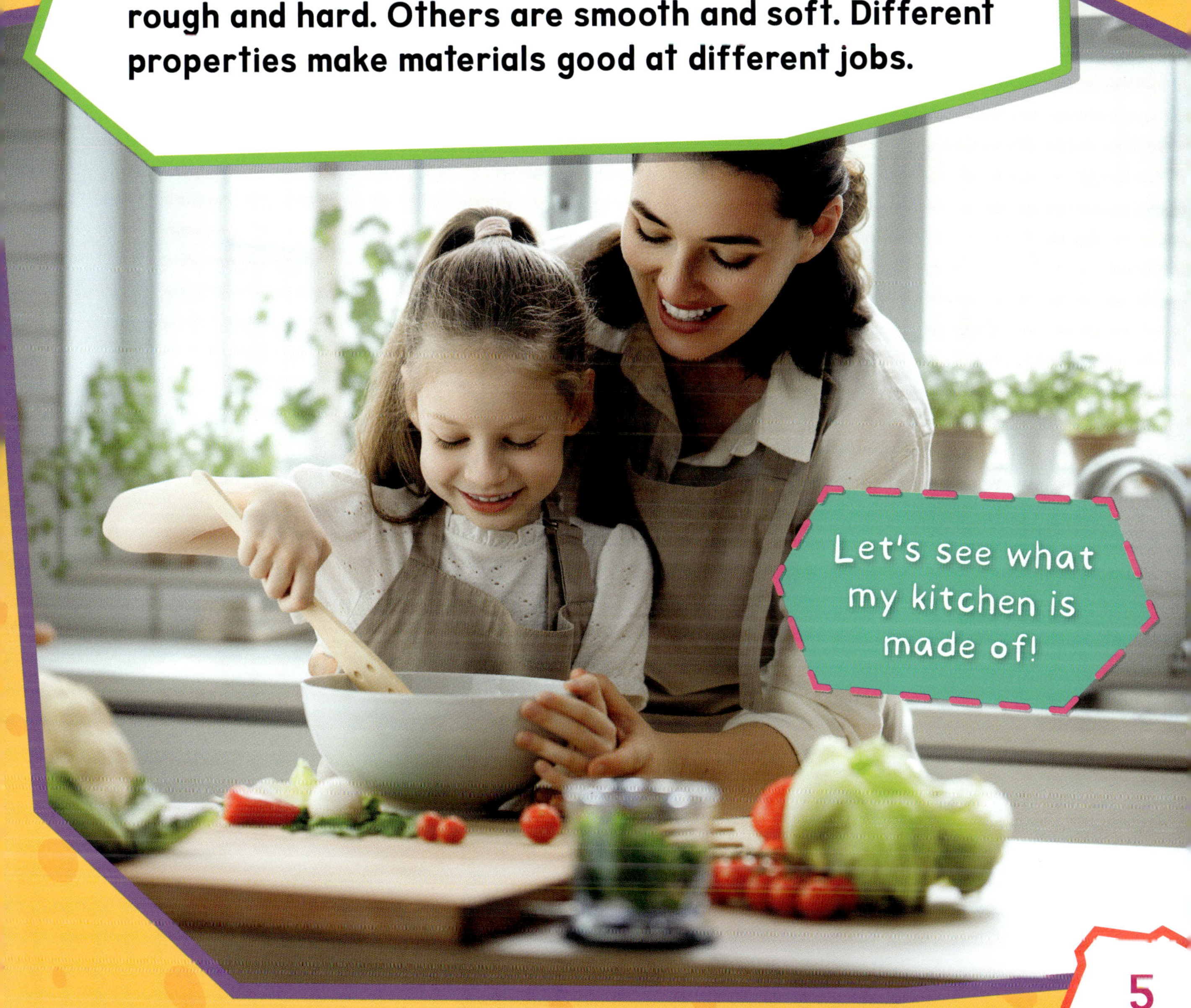

MY FRIDGE

STEEL

My fridge is mostly made of steel. Steel is a human-made material. But it is formed from natural metals. Steel is a durable material that can cope with a lot of use.

My fridge has rubber on the inside of the door. Rubber is flexible. It lines the door with an air-tight seal. This keeps it cold inside my fridge.

MY OVEN

My oven is made of different materials that help keep heat in. The oven door is made of glass. Glass is a human-made material that is transparent. You can see through it.

GLASS

Have you watched food cook through an oven door?

The glass used for oven doors is made to handle high levels of heat. This helps to keep the heat inside, so the oven stays at the right temperature.

MY FRYING PAN

My frying pan is made of a material called cast iron. Cast iron is made from natural metals. It can handle high temperatures without melting. It's a useful material for cooking.

IRON

FACT: Cast iron can be easy to clean.

Cast iron is durable. It can be used for many years without getting damaged.

MY SPOON

My spoon is made of wood. Wood is a natural material. Wooden spoons are used in cooking to stir and mix things. Wood is light and easy to hold.

Wood doesn't conduct much heat, which means it doesn't get hot quickly. This makes it safe to hold. However, wood is flammable. It will burn if it touches an open flame.

MY PLATE

CERAMIC

My plate is made of ceramic. Ceramic is a human-made material. It can handle high temperatures without cracking.

Ceramic is smooth. This makes it easy to clean. But it's also fragile. It can break easily. However, ceramic can last a long time if it is handled carefully.

Be careful when handling ceramic plates.

MY

SPONGE

CELLULOSE

My kitchen sponge is made of cellulose. Cellulose is a natural material. It can **absorb** water and soap. This makes it a good material to help clean dishes.

My sponge has two different sides. The rough side is used to clean tougher stains on my dishes. The softer side is used to wipe smooth surfaces.

MY DISH TOWEL

My dish towel is made of cotton. Cotton is a natural material. It is soft and very light. It can wipe across plates and kitchen utensils without damaging them.

COTTON

Cotton can absorb water. It can soak up water from dishes after they are washed. Then the dishes are dry. Dish towels can get dirty, but cotton can be easily washed.

Have you dried something with a dish towel?

SPOT THE

MATERIALS

Which of these objects is made of ceramic?

FORK

CUP

CUTTING BOARD

Only the cup is made of ceramic. The cutting board is made of wood. and the fork is made of metal.

Which of these objects is made of wood?

KITCHEN CUPBOARD

DRINKING GLASS

KNIFE

Only the cupboard is made of wood. The knife is made of metal, and the drinking glass is made of glass.

WHAT IS IN YOUR KITCHEN?

There are many materials that make up our kitchens. These materials were all chosen because of their useful properties. Without these properties, the objects would not do their jobs properly.

Your kitchen probably has very similar objects to mine. Some objects might be made of many different materials. Look at something in your kitchen. What is it made of? Why was that material chosen?

GLOSSARY

ABSORB	to take in or soak up
DESCRIBING	saying what something is like
DURABLE	not easily broken or worn out
FLAMMABLE	able to catch fire and burn
NATURAL	found in nature and not made by people
SURFACES	the outside or top layers of things
TEMPERATURE	how hot or cold something is
UTENSILS	tools that are used to do things in the home

INDEX